know
the
game

Short Tennis

by Sue Rich

Produced in collaboration with
The Lawn Tennis Association

Published by A & C Black (Publishers) Ltd
35 Bedford Row, London WC1R 4JH

Contents

Fig. 1 Children assembled for the national finals

Introduction

Short tennis is a mini-form of lawn tennis. It is played on a short tennis court or a badminton court which is the same size. The rackets are made of plastic and there are two types of ball which can be used. The indoor ball is a yellow foam one while the outdoor ball is slightly harder but still less hard than a tennis ball.

The sport is mostly for young children just beginning ball and racket games but is a good teaching aid for older children. Adults can also have great fun playing the game; it is a sport for all the family.

The game was first introduced into this country in 1979 by Lawn Tennis Association officials. They realised the enormous potential of short tennis after seeing demonstrations of the game in Sweden. A pilot study was launched in the Eastern Region in 1980 and, following the success of this scheme, short tennis was officially launched by the LTA on a nationwide basis on 7 May 1982.

Anyone trying the game immediately realises how much fun and realism it offers. A 6–10 year-old can learn basic ball sense and ball awareness, as well as all the racket and ball skills of lawn tennis, without the problems that lawn tennis sometimes presents for young children, such as the court being too big, the racket unwieldy and the balls bouncing too high and fast. Short tennis removes these obstacles.

Each year more and more children are being introduced to short tennis and many, who would probably not have played but for short tennis, are now not only playing tennis but are appearing in tournaments and are even selected for regional and national training squads.

Organization of short tennis

The Lawn Tennis Association is the governing body for short tennis in this country, and the department which is directly concerned with the organization of the game is the National Development Department. The address of the Lawn Tennis Association is given on page 32.

Each county has its own short tennis organiser and, in most cases, a Short Tennis Committee who looks after the administration of the game within its county. The name of the short tennis organiser in any particular county can be obtained by contacting the Short Tennis Department of the L.T.A. Each county aims to hold teach-ins showing how short tennis is played and taught and organises an annual tournament open to all 8 years and under players. Most counties hold short tennis tournaments for slightly older children and occasionally even for adults!

There are now many locally arranged inter-school short tennis matches (with ages ranging from 8–11 years) and some counties organise a Schools' Short Tennis League, e.g. Cambridgeshire. There are also inter-county short tennis matches where the emphasis is on a day of fun!

Short tennis is not only played in many primary and secondary schools but also at several tennis clubs, sports centres and village halls, and there are many short tennis clubs now in operation. In the summer months the game is also part of the L.T.A./Prudential Junior Coaching Scheme. There are now numerous places where short tennis can be played – if in doubt contact your county short tennis organiser.

Short tennis is not only confined to county level but is also very much part of Regional and National Development programmes with the annual Regional and National Tournaments and numerous 'road show' presentations.

Fig. 2 A player in the national finals

Fig. 3 Adults can enjoy the game too! (The author)

Fig. 4 The boy and girl winners of the National Short Tennis Finals, Telford 1985

The court

Short tennis is played on a short tennis court 13.4 m × 6.1 m (44' × 20') but can quite easily be played on a badminton court, which is exactly the same size. If played on a badminton court then you must ignore the inner tramlines and imagine the centre line runs throughout the court.

There are also court boundary guidelines:

	General Play	Competition
Minimum run-back	1.8 m (6')	2.6 m (8' 6")
Minimum side-run	1.5 m (5')	2.1 m (7')
Minimum side-run between courts	1.8 m (6')	2.7 m (9')
Minimum unobstructed height over court	4.0 m (13')	5.2 m (17')

When playing outdoors, using the harder 'outdoor' ball (see page 7), larger boundaries are required. Therefore the competition boundary guidelines should be regarded as the minimum measurements for general play.

However, short tennis can easily be played and enjoyed within more restricted boundaries. For example, if a badminton court is used and the baseline (line at the back of the court) is very close to the wall, then the inner line could be used.

The net should be 0.80 m (2' 7") in height at the centre and 0.85 m (2' 9") at the posts.

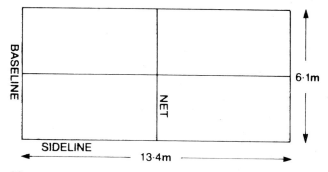

Fig. 5

Equipment and clothing

Equipment

You only need a short tennis racket (or even one of the mini range of tennis rackets) and a ball to play the game.

When playing indoors, a yellow foam ball is used. Outdoors, the foam ball or the harder rubber one can be used. (See Fig. 6)

Clothing

Your normal sports kit is fine to wear for short tennis provided it is comfortable and allows you easy movement. It is best to wear some tennis or gym shoes with good soles.

In competition play you generally have to wear recognised tennis clothing, which is often white in colour. (See Figs. 7 and 8)

Fig. 6

Fig. 7 Suitable clothing for boys

Fig. 8 ...and girls

8

How to start playing

It is important to be able to understand how the ball moves in the air and what the ball does when it hits the ground. Also, you need to get the feel of the racket and the ball together. Here are a few exercises to get you started.

Ball sense exercises without a racket

(a) On your own
  1. Throw the ball (not necessarily a short tennis ball) in the air and catch it—easy. (See Fig. 9)
  2. Now throw the ball in the air, clap your hands and catch it—slightly harder. Try one clap before catching, then two claps, all the way to ten claps—much harder!
  3. Bounce the ball on the ground and catch it with two hands or one hand—easy.
  4. Bounce the ball up and down on the ground with one hand—harder.
  5. Bounce the ball on the ground and move around the court at the same time—harder.
  6. Bounce the ball on the ground in and out of targets—this needs control.
  7. Bounce the ball on the ground, gradually bouncing it lower and lower until you almost touch the ground, and then come up again.

Fig. 9

(b) With a partner/friend

1. Throw the ball underarm to each other and practise catching it after one bounce and also before the bounce.
2. Then start to move each other around—throw some high balls, some low ones, some wide ones. Tennis is all about trying to move to the ball at the right time.

(c) Against a wall

1. Throw the ball against the wall and catch it after one bounce. Try this ten times.
2. Throw the ball against the wall and catch it before the bounce. Try ten of these.
3. Throw the ball against the wall and clap your hands before catching it without letting the ball bounce. Repeat with 2 claps, 3 claps, working up to ten—it's good fun but quite difficult.

Having acquired a feel for the ball, let's now introduce the racket. Try these exercises. (You don't have to do *all* the previous exercises before proceeding to these.)

Racket and ball exercises

1. Bounce the ball on the ground with the racket. Count how many times you can do this. (See Fig. 10)
2. Bounce the ball in the air with the racket. Count how many times you can do this. (See Fig. 11)
3. Bounce the ball on the ground and then in the air.
4. Try bouncing the ball on one face of the racket and then the other face—it's quite difficult to keep this going.
5. If you can master number 4 try 2 bounces on one face of the racket and 2 the other side, then 3 each side, then 4 each side—keep going.
6. Bounce the ball on the ground in and out of targets.
7. You can also try running around bouncing the ball on the ground or in the air. If you do this at school it is great fun in teams—try it.

Fig. 10

Fig. 11

The forehand drive

Having practised a few exercises with the ball and racket, let us now look at the forehand drive.

For a right handed player this is the shot played on the right side of the body after the ball has bounced once.

Let the ball bounce *once* and then *swing* with the racket. Can you hit the ball?

Hint: try to hit the ball at arm's length (that is, at a comfortable distance)—it is much easier.

Practices

1. Try to hit forehands against the wall.
2. Ask a friend to throw you a ball underarm and try to hit it, after the bounce, back over the net. Out of 10 throws see how many you can hit over the net and into court.
3. As you improve you will be able to rally—that is when you and a friend keep hitting the ball over the net without stopping. See how many times you can do this.

(See Fig. 12 and front cover)

Fig. 12 Forehand drive (right hander)

The backhand drive

For a right handed player, this is the shot you play on the left side of your body after the ball has bounced once.

You can play the backhand with one or two hands holding the racket.

If you play double handed, you have to be quicker on your feet as you do not have as much reach.

The backhand drive is played like the forehand. So again, you *swing* with the racket and hit the ball a comfortable distance away from yourself. Try a low to high swing, it is much easier.

Hint: good backhands are played with a lot of shoulder turn in the preparation.

Try the same practices as you did on the forehand drive.
(See Figs. 13 and 15)

Fig. 13 Two handed backhand (right hander)

Fig. 14 Forehand drive (left hander)

Fig. 15 One handed backhand (left hander)

The service

The game begins with the service so you must learn how to play this stroke. You can either serve underarm or overarm.

Underarm serve

This is the easier of the two serves. It is played like the forehand except that you do not let the ball bounce. Hit the ball at your side.

Fig. 16 Underarm serve

Overarm serve

This service is more difficult to learn but is a far better method once you can do it. To begin with you should stand sideways. Then place the ball in the air with one hand and throw the racket head at it with the other hand—don't let go of the racket, though! The ball is hit above your head and slightly in front of your body.

Hint: the service has the same action as the overarm throw.

Practice
Try the overarm serve over the net or above a line marked on a wall. If in difficulty, play the underarm serve. When you begin playing matches, try the first serve overarm and the second serve underarm.

Fig. 17 Overarm serve

The volley

The volley is the name we give to the stroke played before the ball bounces. Generally it is played from close to the net. Try to **block** the ball when you volley, or bring the racket forward in a short, sharp movement as if you are punching the ball.

Hint: for good volleys, try not to take the racket back too far and don't follow through too much. Move forward to the ball and grip the racket firmly.

Practices
1. Ask your friend to throw you a ball at about shoulder height, and try to volley the ball back to him/her.
2. Try to rally with your friend—he/she hits the ball from the back of the court and you volley at the net—good fun.
3. As you improve, try a rally of volleys to each other. You can do this over the net or in an open space. Ten is a good score.

(See Figs. 18 and 19)

Fig. 18 Forehand volley

Fig. 19 Backhand volley

How to play the game

Singles

This is for two players only. The game starts with one player (A) serving from behind the baseline and one player (B) returning the serve.

The server (A), standing behind the baseline, serves (underarm or overarm) first, from the right court, and the ball has to land anywhere in the area X (the diagonal half of the opponent's court). This is shown in the diagram. If it does not land in this area then it is a fault and you are allowed a second try. If this one fails you lose the point—double fault. If the serve strikes the top of the net and falls into the correct area it is called a 'let' and you take this serve again. If the ball lands in area X then player (B) returns the ball after the bounce and the game continues until somebody wins the point. If player B strikes the served ball before the bounce he loses the point. After the first point, the player (A) then serves from the left court and so on from alternate sides. Once the ball is in play (after the return of service) the players may strike the ball either before or after the bounce. (See Fig. 21)

Fig. 20 Singles match

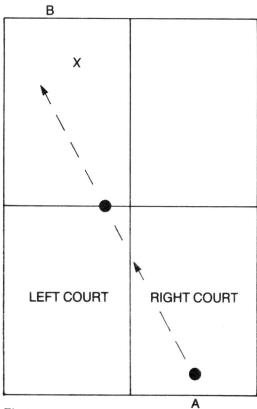

B

X

LEFT COURT   RIGHT COURT

A

Fig. 21

In the 'first to 11' points scoring method, the service changes after every 2 points. After 8 points have been played, the players change ends.

Doubles

This is for four players with a team of 2 players each side of the net. Play is like that in singles, except that the four players each serve for 2 points in rotation.

For example, player (A) serves 2 points, then player (C) or (D) from the opposing team, then player (B), then (C) or (D) (whoever didn't serve the first time).

Fig. 22 Doubles match

Winning points and scoring

The scoring system for short tennis is the 'first to 11 points', with the score called out in numbers 1, 2, 3, etc. If the score reaches 10 points all, then the match continues until one player has a lead of 2 points such as 13–11 or 15–13.

This scoring system makes it easier to introduce competition for very young children. It is also convenient when there is a time limitation. You can easily use a different scoring system, for example, 'first to 9 points' to suit the individual circumstances.

In tournament play a proper scoring sheet is used. Scoring pads are obtainable from the L.T.A.(See Fig. 23)

Short tennis is also a very easy way to introduce the proper lawn tennis scoring method.

Let us look at how you can *win points*.

If you serve so well that your opponent cannot return the ball at all, or cannot return the ball into court, you win the point. Don't forget—any ball which lands on a line is counted as 'in'.

Once the game has started, you win the point if your opponent lets the ball bounce twice, so it a good idea to try to make your opponent run around so that he cannot get to the ball in time!

By good play, you might force your opponent to hit the ball into the net or out of court so that you win the point. Again, making your opponent move around forwards, backwards and sideways, might cause him or her to make a mistake.

If you force your opponent to hit the ball onto a wall or the ceiling before it lands in your half of the court, you will win the point.

Finally, you can win the point when your opponent serves 2 faults in a row!

Here are some useful ideas to help you win points:
(a) make your opponent run around using all the court;
(b) try to play onto his or her weaker side—often this is the backhand;
(c) as soon as you have played a shot get ready for the next one—don't stand and admire your good shot;
(d) try to get to the net—it is great fun playing at the net too;
(e) Finally, never give up; keep going!

SHORT TENNIS SCORE SHEET

Event _St. Johns School Tournament (Boys - 8 & Under)_ Court **3**

Players _Peter GREEN_ v _John BROWN_

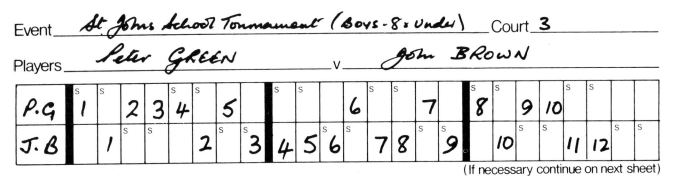

(If necessary continue on next sheet)

Winner _____ J. BROWN

Score _____ 12 - 10.

1. Enter initials of player serving first
   in top box. Thereafter S indicates server.

2. Players change ends every 8 points.

Fig. 23

Some further practices

Hopefully, you have already tried out the practices in the book. The aim here is to give you a few more ideas to help improve your game.

Forehands and backhands (ground strokes)

1. In order to try to hit the ball deep, place a target, e.g. mat, on the court. You and your partner can then rally, aiming for the targets. If you are both right handed, try standing as in the diagram above so you can hit cross court forehands to each other. Don't forget, when you play matches, a deep ball makes it harder for your opponent to hit a good return. This practice can be repeated, if the targets are moved to the opposite side, with backhands. (See Fig. 24)

PATH OF BALL

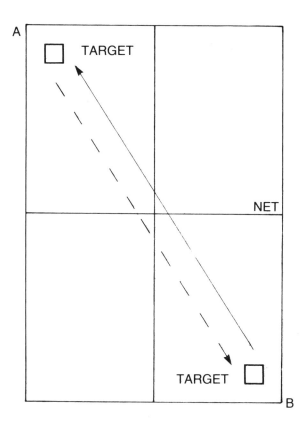

Fig. 24

2. Now place the targets opposite each other as in the diagram below and try rallying straight so that one person hits forehands while the other hits backhands (if you are both right handed). After a while change ends so that you can practise the opposite shot.
(See Fig. 25)

3. Another fun exercise is when you and your partner are both running from side to side.
Player A hits straight while player B hits cross court. Try a rally of 20 or 30—this can be quite tiring. After a while change roles so player A hits cross court and player B hits straight.
(See Fig. 26)

PATH OF BALL

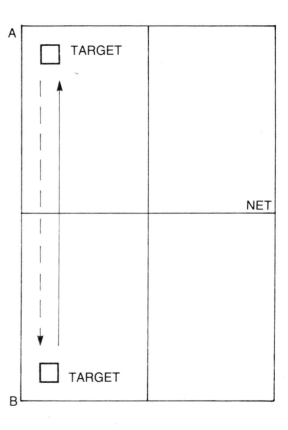

Fig. 25

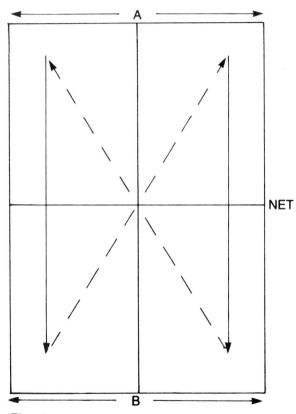

Fig. 26

Linking groundstrokes and volleys

Once you have a feel for the volley there is nothing like putting the groundstrokes and the volleys together.

4. Try the 3 ball exercise.
   One person feeds 3 balls from mid court; the first ball is deep and A plays a groundstroke, the second ball is short and A plays another groundstroke (called an approach shot) as he moves to the net, and the third ball is fed as a volley. Great fun. As you get better you could do this with one ball only. (See Fig. 27)

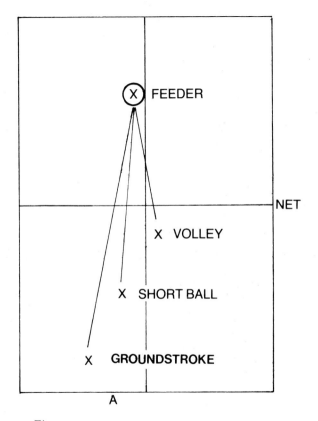

FEEDER

NET

X VOLLEY

X SHORT BALL

X GROUNDSTROKE

A

Fig. 27

Tournaments

Once you have a feel for the game of short tennis there is nothing more exciting than playing in a tournament. Here you get the chance to meet other people interested in short tennis and to try your talent against theirs.

Every county in Britain now holds a *Short Tennis Tournament* each year, some time during the period January–March. There is a special event for those children 8 years and under (under 8 years on 31 December of the previous year), and the most successful of these progress to a regional tournament. Most counties, however, do not restrict their tournaments to this age level only and include events for 9 years and under, 10 years and under and other age levels.

The tournaments are generally organised on a *round-robin* basis. This means that all the children are divided into groups, so you can be assured of at least a few games of short tennis even if you lose them all! Consider, for example, an entry of 16 players. We could divide the competitors into 4 groups, each of 4 players.

Each person then plays 3 matches. Depending on the format for the event, the winner of each group might progress to the semi-finals which is then a knock-out (that is, if you lose now you are out!) or the winner and

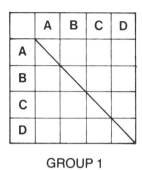

GROUP 1

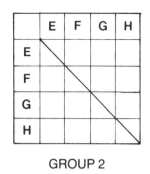

GROUP 2

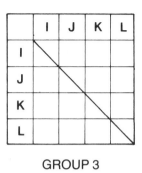

GROUP 3

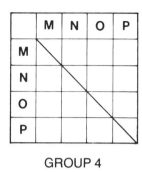

GROUP 4

Fig. 28

KNOCKOUT STAGE

runner-up in each group might progress to the next stage. Whatever the format, you would be told before the tournament started.

Some counties hold more than one tournament a year and now there are often tournaments run locally at sports centres, clubs etc., so look out for the posters!

If you are 8 years or under and are successful in your county tournament, you will be invited to the *regional tournament* which takes place in March or April. Here you would play against other children who have also been successful in their own county. The competition now gets harder—still great fun though!

If you are lucky and good enough to do well in the regional tournament, you might be invited to play in the

Fig. 29 National Finals

national finals which are held in June each year. Here the emphasis is still on lots of activity and fun with everybody gaining some form of prize. Both the regional and national events are also played largely on a round robin basis.

You can find out about tournaments by contacting the Lawn Tennis Association who will in turn put you in contact with your county short tennis organiser.

Where do we go from here?

Short tennis is just the start of years of fun with a ball and a racket. Once you have mastered the basic skills of short tennis there is no greater challenge than trying the real game of tennis. The real game is played on a larger court with slightly different line markings and with a higher net. The rackets are different and the balls are harder.

I suggest you play on the large court with a small tennis racket (not too heavy and not too long) and use the foam short tennis ball a few times. Later on, have a go with the tennis racket and the harder, outdoor, short tennis ball. Finally, try the tennis racket and the tennis ball—now you're there!

Hint: try lowering the tennis net to start with if you are having difficulty and playing only in the service boxes.

Short tennis is great fun indoors on those cold winter days but it is particularly enjoyable to play on an outdoor tennis court on a warm day in the summer.

Once you have tried the real game of tennis it is a good idea to sign on for a tennis course for beginners, and there is no better way to start than at an L.T.A./Prudential Open Centre. Every county organises lots of these centres each summer and each course is for one hour a week for 6 weeks at a very modest cost.

If you enjoy tennis, the next step is to join a tennis club where you can play all the year round. A tennis club is a super way to meet lots of other people who enjoy tennis and also gives you a place where you can practise. There are also L.T.A./Prudential Junior Playing Centres in many parts of the country now where you can go and play.

Your school is another place where you might be able to play tennis and there are also the local parks and leisure centres. Information about tennis in your area can be obtained from your county L.T.A. Secretary (the L.T.A. will supply addresses).

Once you start to master the game, then, of course, there are tennis tournaments you can play in and—who

Fig. 30 Boris Becker, Wimbledon champion 1985

knows—one day it could be Wimbledon that is your next tournament.

So you see, short tennis is the ideal start to a sport you can enjoy for the rest of your life—don't forget it is fun!

Addresses

The Lawn Tennis Association
Barons Court
West Kensington
London W14 9EG Tel: 01 385 2366

Short Tennis equipment is exclusively marketed and distributed by
Slazenger Racket Sports
Challenge House
Mitcham Road
Croydon
Surrey CR9 3AU

Similar equipment can be purchased from
Mini Tennis Limited
The Hollies
Station Road
West Dereham
King's Lynn, Norfolk PE33 9RR

Further Information

The Lawn Tennis Association is introducing a Short Tennis Instruction Course for potential teachers of short tennis. Details may be obtained from your regional office (addresses from the L.T.A.).

Details of short tennis booklets, videos and other merchandise are available from the L.T.A.

Acknowledgements

The authors and publishers wish to thank Brian Blincoe, L.T.A. Director of National Development, and Charles Applewhaite, L.T.A. Director of Coaching, for their valuable assistance in preparing this book.

Photographs by courtesy of Tommy Hindley, L.T.A. official photographer. All, except Fig. 30, taken at the Daily Mail 1985 Short Tennis Championships national final at Telford Racquet and Fitness Centre (for children 8 years and under).